FINANCIAL KNOWLEDGE FOR WEALTH CREATION

Drawing the Line between Your Needs and Wants

BY

RAYMOND L. BAEZ, WARREN I. JAYNE

COPYRIGHT©2020

COPYRIGHT

No part of this, publication may be reproduced, distributed, or transmitted in any form or by any means, including photocopy, recording or other electronic or mechanical methods, or by any information storage and retrieval system without the prior written permission of the publisher, except in a case of very brief quotations embodied in critical reviews and certain other noncommercial uses per-mitted by copyright law.

TABLE OF CONTENT

CHAPTER 1

BECOMING FINANCIALLY LITERATE

CHAPTER 2

WHEN THE MONEY STOPS COMING; WHAT HAPPENS?

CHAPTER 3

THE LINE BETWEEN NEEDS AND WANTS

CHAPTER 4

NEEDS

CHAPTER 5

WANTS

CHAPTER 6

THE NEW WORLD'S INCOME

CHAPTER 7

BORROWING, LOANS AND DEBTS

CHAPTER 8

THE REAL TRIP TO FINANCIAL FREEDOM

THE END

CHAPTER 1

BECOMING FINANCIALLY LITERATE

Being financially literate goes way beyond being educated or taking one or two courses on some professional financial courses. It even goes beyond knowing how to make good figures and amassing wealth. It's beyond going through the four (4) corners of some higher institution and coming out with some degrees and qualifications on financially related disciplines.

All of the above are all valid means of gaining financial knowledge and understanding, but, financial literacy is more about having in your grasp "adequate and sufficient knowledge on managing your finances, deciding what will or not help your finances, best saving models and good investment strategies.

Becoming really financially literate is more about knowing where, when and how to draw the line at every time between what's important or necessary, good or better, lasting or passive, sustaining or entertaining, or whether if it's just a want or need.

All of the above mentioned points in paragraph 1, are places where one can acquire some knowledge, there are even some institutions who pride themselves of being champions in Financial Literacy Education. They may be right, but, unless you make a deliberate attempt and moves to gain and utilize this knowledge, then what you have cannot be described as financial literacy.

In this book, you will be shown the right way to achieving and sustaining financial freedom, financial independence, and you will be shown the various ways of determining what actions or ventures will be gainful and yield the required financial result and at the right time.

There will be an elaborate study on making the decision between needs and wants at every point in time; especially as it concerns your financial life.

This is therefore a book recommended for all classes and levels of individuals; but especially for those on salary jobs. Life isn't supposed to end at retirement, but should be better and enjoyable.

CHAPTER 2

WHEN THE MONEY STOPS COMING; WHAT HAPPENS?

This might be a very difficult question for some to come to terms with. It could even become disagreeing or unacceptable to the individuals as at the time of this question and might result to dispute between the individuals.

However one might decide to or instinctively react to the above question, the realistic fact remains that if precise precautionary measures are not taken seriously; the reality of that questions becomes in evitable.

Survey by Standard Chartered, in their analysis on the importance of Financial Literacy in one of their documents in 2017, stated that out of 100 people at retirement:

1. 49 will be dependent on family and charity.
2. 29 will be dead soon after
3. 12 will be broke soon
4. 5 will go back to working thereafter
5. 4 will become financially independent
6. 1 will be rich

Now the big question that begs to be answered is "who will you be in the above list?"

Do you now understand why that question was asked at the beginning of this chapter?

Is it clear to you now that that reality is as it is inevitable and demands answers?

It's however very possible and valid to say that the difference between those in categories 1 – 5 and their associates in categories 5 & 6 could be one or some of the reasons we will discuss later on in this book, or just summed up to say that those set of people are not Financially Literate.

Understanding the fact that all of them worked together at the same time and receiving the same salary, gratuity and pension; what then could possibly be their excuses for not coming out reach or at least financially independent after such a remarkably longtime in service? Here our previous answer comes back again; it's because they do not have adequate knowledge of what to do, when to do it and how to best to go about it that will not turn out to be financially detrimental to them.

Having said that, in putting it in a much simpler term, the whole thing could just be narrowed down to not being able to draw that line between NEEDS and WANTS.

CHAPTER 3

THE LINE BETWEEN NEEDS AND WANTS

As we have already earlier established that the one of the core determinants of a man's financial standing in the long run might be his level of knowledge, understanding and enlightenment as regards to is Needs and Wants. More so to his advantage and overall benefit is his ability to decide which is or is not.

Most times we get so carried away that we can no longer decide or say for sure what wants are worth our time and money. It may seem very important now and look like everything depends on it; but what happens after one week or one month? That commodity that seemed like life depended on it, becomes most painfully a liability. Unable to add any lasting value or importance the person who posses it.

It is therefore pertinent that we explain, discuss about and understand what is important, necessary or essential, or all three at once. So as to act as our decoy at every time we attempt to make that seemingly all important decision; to make sure we do not suffer regrets in the near future.

Let's now see a basic definition of what a need or want is and what makes them different.

NEEDS: these are things that are necessary and essential for one to continue living. That's is to say, if these needs are deprived or not met, and as at the time needed, it may result to the acute suffering, pain, death or possible extinction of the person, animal or living organisms in general.

WANTS: these are things that are good and important for the comfort and entertainment of the person, animal or living organism, at a particular time or period, but not necessarily essential for their sustenance and continuous existence. Meaning that deprivations from wants can in no way lead to the death or extinction of any person or species as they are most times optional.

Many persons, even with their flare for saving and knowledge for investing still find themselves in the same spot they where, unable to make any remarkable progress because of this very simple and basic knowledge of what is important enough to be considered a Need or Want.

It's therefore important at this point that we create a clear and glaring dichotomy to put each in its rightful place.

CHAPTER 4

NEEDS

We have talked about needs in the previous pages; and how they are not just good, but important, relevant, necessary and essential to the overall continuous existence and sustainability of the individual(s) or species as the case may be.

Needs are like the most essential wants in ones diary or budget (we will discuss about this subsequently). It's therefore important to think, strategize, evaluate and re-evaluate before regarding a want as a need.

It's therefore valid to say that, according many facts available, "needs are wants with long term or lasting benefits."

There are different categories of 'NEEDS' that are known. These categories are classified based on their overall functionality in the life of the individual(s).

Below is a diagram of MASLOW'S HIERACHY OF NEEDS. An analogy that explains the categories of human needs I relation to their importance or relevance.

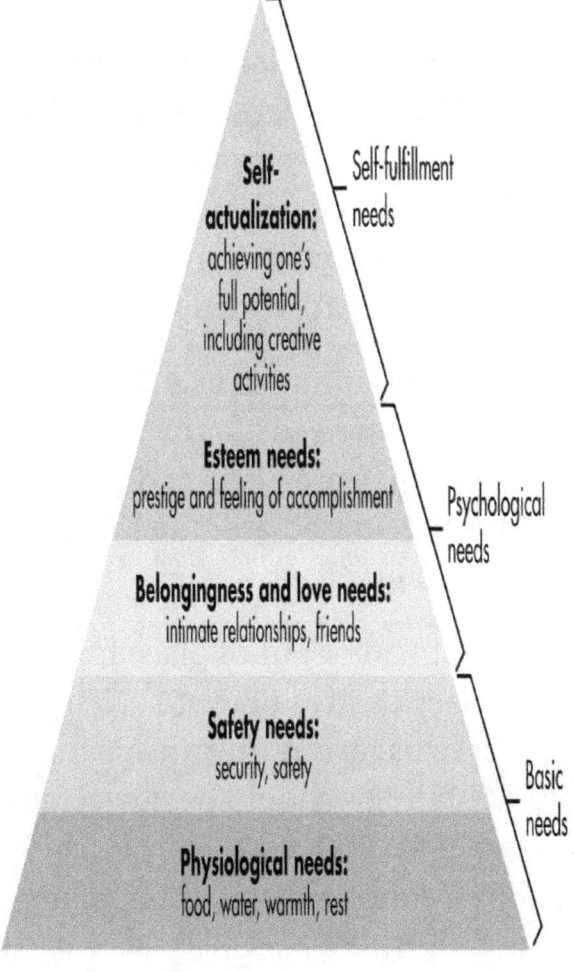

CHAPTER 5

WANTS

We have also tried to explain and describe what 'WANTS' are, in relation to 'NEEDS'. Wants are not bad or irrelevant cravings or desires as it might seem from the previous definitions and descriptions given. They are instead short term gratifying needs.

Wants, though might not be exactly what an individual or person needs for overall sustenance, but they are also good and important for the immediate satisfaction of the individual(s) involved.

As such, it's not bad or out of place in any way to give in to ones desires of wants. Neither does this work suggest by any means that wants are wasteful or should be neglected or left unattended to. Instead wants should be thought about, contemplated upon, managed and decided wish is worthy to be regarded to as need(s).

It's therefore advised that at most point in time a scale of preferences should be made, so as to clearly ascertain what and which of the stated commodities or choices are worthy to be regarded as needs. When this decision is made considering the importance, essentiality and sustainability of these desires, a want can then be seen as a need.

CHAPTER 6

THE NEW WORLD'S INCOME

Any person anywhere around the world can easily tell that things and trends are changing very fast; life has become more complicating, goods and services are now more expensive, efforts outweigh incomes, demands are rising by the second, technology is speedily growing, computers are taking over human jobs and needs are becoming even more difficult to provide. All of these are happening very fast and nothing seems to be changing for the better following the old ways of doing things.

Have you ever had time to check out how employees on particular salary routines live or manage through the month? The accumulating expenses, piling utility and domestic bills and ever stagnant salary payment schedule system. Someone once said "salaries are like hormones, unpredictable at times with imbalances"

One thing that is and may not quickly change is the fact that the price of commodities may rise quickly as demands will, expenses will change from being a little high, to being double the price it was a moment back. Salaries are exhausted even before the seventh (7th) day of the preceding month and more are even borrowed to help meet up with the ever growing demands of family, relatives and self; but in all of these, one thing that will however not easily change is the "salary."

What then can we do to change this unbeneficial process and mode of doing things? What actions can we take to ensure that this circle of lack and unpleasantness? The answer is simple we need to identify and utilize new means of generating residual incomes, and this is by delving conscientiously into the available alternative incomes with the mindset of a winner.

Over the last decade, the world has noticed a paradigm shift from the supposed normal ways of doing things. People have realized that the formal normal isn't so normal after all and as such are delving into the current normal way of generating incomes. And two among the few categories of available options are Crypto currency and Network Marketing.

The introduction of Bitcoin about a decade ago is one of the best things that have happened to the world. At first, some people like me didn't take it serious; but imagine my surprise and disappointment together when I got to know the value of that crypto currency few years ago.

Network marketing on its own is a 'people helping people grow and growing themselves in the process." You cannot count how many persons who now have millions of dollars in their possession all over the world from network marketing. For copyright and advertisement laws, I shall not be mentioning names, but explore the internet and the goldmine staring at us.

CHAPTER 7

BORROWING, LOANS AND DEBTS

It's almost impossible for one to live through these times without falling into any of the following; 'borrowing, loans and debt." Almost impossible because it could be avoided or controlled as much as possible.

Borrowing has become a part of the normal present day lifestyle; it's become so easy that the creditor does not even have to know you personally before giving out the money. The system has made all of these possible and stress-free. People now borrow and take loans easily, with very good, attractive and convenient payment methods designed to keep you indebted for as long as possible.

Have you thought about your credit card and how much of a help it really is? Yes, it's convenient and you can get all the things you want, when you want them and how you want them without worrying so much that you are yet receive your salary. Take note of the word "want" and not "need" as the case may be. Now let's take a look at all the ways you lose your money through your credit card:

PAYMENTS INVOLVED

MAXIMUM AMOUNT DUE: Total outstanding credit card balance

MINIMUM AMOUNT DUE: A percent of your credit card outstanding balance + All charges+All fees+Interest for the month+Arrears.

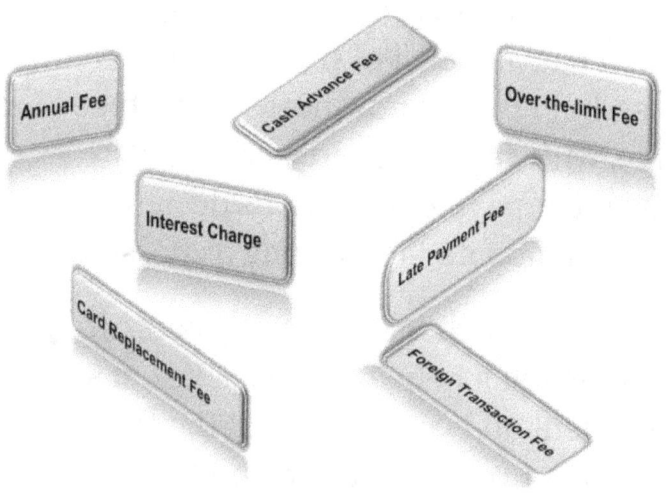

What the above diagram gotten from Standard Chartered signifies here is that we spend so much more without even knowing it.

Some people are in the habit of taking loans; but the thing however is if these loans are taken for something considered want or need (from our previous pages). The point here is that people prefer to take loans for things that their values won't last and do not generate or bring any long term income, instead of taking those loans for investments and ventures that will generate long term income. In fact that is what differentiates a bad debt from a good one.

Next time before you buy that phone, car or any other item that you believe to be important to you, take out time to ask yourself if that will generate you the desired long term income to give you that dream life; in other words, find out if that your desire is just a "want" or "need."

There's no need to get yourself indebted so much for nothing, "think it through over and over again before making that decision to buy that thing you think you so much desire."

CHAPTER 8

THE REAL TRIP TO FINANCIAL FREEDOM

Becoming financially free is a deliberate act with careful planning and systematic efforts. These questions at this time should be considered if one wish to grow from this stage of constantly being broke to one of wealth and comfort.

1.) What do you do before the money comes?
2.) What's the first thing you do when the money comes?
3.) Are you rigid or flexible in your spending?
4.) Does it finish before start looking for alternatives?

The above questions are very important for anyone who desires to break from the normal routine of scarcity and lacks. We are however going to treat the questions above as points, and I hope you are putting yourself in that position to evaluate and discover if you have been your own problem all the while.

WHAT DO YOU DO BEFORE THE MONEY COMES?

What this question demands to know is if you plan your day, week, month and possibly year. If you haven't started doing "budgeting," then I recommend you begin right away. It's only by doing this that you can actually control your money when it comes; otherwise, your money controls you.

> Why do you think organizations, establishments and even nations have budget before the year if not to act as a guide through the year; to save them from unnecessary and costly expenditures.

Let's see some tips on how you can start your own impeccable budgeting:

STANDARD CHARTERED BUDGETING TEMPLATE

Exp. Income	Month 1	Month 2	Month 3
Balance brought forward			
Salary			
Business income Investment income			
EXPENDITURES			
Food			
Fuel/Transport			
Rent			
School fees			
Clothing			
Entertainment			
Donations/tithe			
Investment			
Balance			

WHAT'S THE FIRST THING YOU DO WHEN THE MONEY COMES?

This question may sound trivial to you, but it's in fact very important in the journey to financial freedom.

- Do you start buying all the beautiful things you've always wanted, paying all your debts, donating to charity and spending as it comes to mind?
- Or do you save/invest, follow your budget and plan for rainy days?

I tell you that the difference between both persons is that the first will save/invest whatever is left, while the second will spend whatever is remaining after saving/investing. Now tell me, in a few years, which of these two will be living more comfortable? I guess you know the answer as much as I do.

HOW TO WISELY ALLOCATE MONEY

PARTICULAR	ALLOCATION	INCOME: 100K
Savings	10%	10,000
Transport/Entertainment	10%	10,000
Housing	20%	20,000
Food	10%	10,000
School fees	20%	20,000
Medical	10%	10,000
Investment	10%	10,000
Emergency	10%	10,000

Once you have done the above, it's now left for you to decide from where you have leftovers for that month and how best to spend it.

ARE YOU RIGID OR FLEXIBLE IN YOUR SPENDING?

"Wisdom is profitable to direct...," The great book says. Spending as budgeted is one of the best ways to get good results; it will be however unwise not to recognize extreme cases and know when to bend a little for over all good.

DOES IT FINISH BEFORE YOU START LOOKING FOR ALTERNATIVES?

From the moment the first money comes, start making efforts for another. That is why we talked about alternative sources of income.

This book will not talk further about preferred or tested alternative means of income at the moment, but advice you make a research on your own, seek professional advice and wait for my next book.

THE END

www.ingramcontent.com/pod-product-compliance
Lightning Source LLC
Chambersburg PA
CBHW070909220526
45466CB00005B/2184